A Green Deal for the Manchester–Mersey Bioregion

Mark Burton

GreenDealManchester

http://greendealmanchester.wordpress.com/

Manchester: 2009

A Green Deal for the Manchester-Mersey Bioregion

Mark H Burton

Manchester 2009

ISBN 978-1-4457-8342-0

Contents

A Green Deal for the Manchester–Mersey Bioregion

Introduction

We are living in unprecedented times. At least three linked crises are coming together to threaten not only our accustomed standard of living and financial security, but also the resource base of the late 20th century economy and way of life, *and* the capacity and integrity of the earth's natural systems on which we all depend.

This conjuncture of crises requires urgent and drastic action– if it is already not too late – that completely restructures the way we organise to produce and distribute the things we need to have worthwhile lives, and do this fairly and sustainably. *Appendix 3: What are the crises and what has caused them?* sets out one high level analysis of the causes and nature of this combination of crises.

The following outline tries to set out a programme of action at a regional level of analysis – using the example of what we are calling the Manchester–Mersey bioregion.

Under-utilised and unused land, Collyhurst and Greenheys, Manchester.

Context

The New Green Deal and the replacement economy.

"The global economy is facing a 'triple crunch'. It is a combination of a credit-fuelled financial crisis, accelerating climate change and soaring energy prices underpinned by an encroaching peak in oil production. These three overlapping events threaten to develop into a perfect storm, the like of which has not been seen since the Great Depression. To help prevent this from happening we are proposing a Green New Deal."[1]

The New Green Deal (NGD) pamphlet was issued in summer 2008 by the New Economics Foundation (NEF)[2]. It was prescient given the accelerating impact and predictions of climate change and the deepening economic crisis resulting from the bursting of the financial speculative bubbles. NEF NGD identifies a the third problem area, the energy crunch: which properly stated is not just the approaching scarcity of oil (which is at or near world peak production now) but also the pressing need to stop basing the economy on fossil hydrocarbons altogether.

The NEF NGD attempts to address this trio of threats in an integrated way. That it is not entirely successful[3] is not really the point – these problem areas define the context for any alternative approach. The NGD outlines a kind of green Keynesian approach: sustainable development with social justice. It fails to fully recognise that the trio of problems is the combination of the latest crisis in capitalist accumulation with the planetary limits to capitalism[4]. But we can use it as a starting point for collectively planning for both resilience to shocks and also for a more adequate and sustainable approach to human development. This has to happen at local[5], regional, national and international[6] levels. Key to this is the idea of a

---

[1] New Economics Foundation, A *Green New Deal. Joined-up policies to solve the triple crunch of the credit crisis, climate change and high oil prices: The first report of the Green New Deal Group,* 2008. See *Appendix 1: The NEF New Green Deal, its proposals.*

[2] See note 1.

[3] See note 4 and the critique by Sean Thompson, now posted at various sites including http://another-green-world.blogspot.com/2008/10/green-keynesianism-and-its-limits-by.html and http://liammacuaid.wordpress.com/2008/11/09/the-green-new-deal-sean-thompson/.

[4] See *Appendix 3: What are the crises and what has caused them?* for an analysis of the present crises that identifies the need for a more fundamental rebuild of the economy than the NEF authors.

[5] The level at which some of the most innovative work is focussing, see for example Hopkins, R. (2008). *The Transition Handbook: From Oil Dependency to Local resilience.* Totnes: Green Books. Also at http://www.appropedia.org/TTH: Introduction and Lerch, D (2007) Post Carbon Cities:Planning for energy and climate uncertainty. Sebastopol USA: Post carbon press (abridged version on line at http://www.postcarboncities.net/).

[6] See the United Nations Environment Programme initiatives: A *Global Green Deal* and *Towards a Green Economy* http://www.unep.org

replacement economy to take the place of both the finance bubble economy and the economy of real production and distribution that is not only unsustainable but hurrying the ecosystem to destruction[7].

The Manchester–Mersey bioregion

"Archaeology records a series of civilisations that rose and fell as they depleted their bioregional resource base."[8]

The North West's major city, Manchester, and the area around it has been variously identified and described as Greater Manchester, a city region and together with other areas (Lancashire, Cheshire and Merseyside) as the North West. It has been a dynamic region economically and is home to several million people (depending on where we draw the boundaries). Current economic orthodoxy sees its future development in terms of certain key sectors: advanced engineering and materials, biomedical, business and professional services, construction, creative and digital industries, energy and environmental technologies, food and drink[9]. This all needs rethinking in the context of the triple crisis of climate change, decarbonisation/energy crunch, and the collapse of the financial / neoliberal accumulation regime. Because of the imperatives of reducing energy expenditure and (re)generating a real local economy it is at the regional level that transformative green strategies can make the most sense. It is unsustainable to import our food and our sources of wealth from outside the region. Some needs will have to be met from imports and trade but a principle of subsidiarity needs to be applied – only bring in those things that are both necessary and cannot be sourced or made locally[10]. Yet it is difficult to see how most needs could be met within a small local area. It may therefore make most sense to think of the region

---

[7] It is now becoming ever clearer that previous predictions of global warming have underestimated the non-linear effects, for example the positive feedback effects of the reduction of reflective polar ice and the methane-releasing destruction of wetlands and tundra.

[8] Holmgren, D. (2008) Future Scenarios: Mapping the cultural implications of peak oil and climate change. http://www.futurescenarios.org/ or contact publisher at http://tinyurl.com/d7yd4v

[9] The Northwest Regional Development Agency http://www.englandsnorthwest.com/invest/travel-and-infrastructure.html

[10] A concept developed in some detail at the beginning of the 20th century by P. A. Kropotkin, *Fields, factories, and workshops; or, Industry combined with agriculture and brain work with manual work* (New, rev., and enl. ed.). New York and London,: Thomas Nelson & Sons, 1912, although he did not use this term. There will of course still be relationships with other parts of the world. These will involve necessary trade, sharing of knowledge and solidarity. Moreover in our relatively fortunate situation we have an ongoing responsibility to some producers as a result of the distortion of agriculture and other production over the years of colonial and postcolonial domination – thus Windward Island bananas might still be imported (by hi-tech sailing ship?) while aid is given to enable that bioregion to endogenously develop in its own right.

as a "bioregion" – for example the area of the Mersey watershed, wherein there is potentially sufficient diversity of ecologies and natural resources – which will in turn have to be safeguarded and repaired to secure the sustenance for human settlement[11]. As the crises bite and radical actions take place, the present focus on the North West region, or the Northern Way, or the Manchester City Region will have to be supplanted by a focus on the bioregion which holds the keys to sustainable living under conditions of energy austerity.

Our bioregion is diverse, with areas of urban sprawl, rich farmland in Cheshire and Lancashire, forest and woodland, heath and moorland, west – facing Pennine slopes, built-up estuary and coastal plain. It contains many of the resources that we will need for regional self-sufficiency. We need to get to know and understand it better[12].

---

[11] The concept of bioregion has been used widely in permaculture. Bill Mollison (*Permaculture: A designer's manual.* Tyalgum, NSW: Tagari, 1988) defines it in terms of populations of from 7,000 to 40,000 – considerably smaller than that of the urban-centred region considered here but other writers have used to refer to regions with populations of several million.

[12] There is brief summary of the main features of the bioregion from the Environment Agency http://www.environment-agency.gov.uk/research/planning/33192.aspx

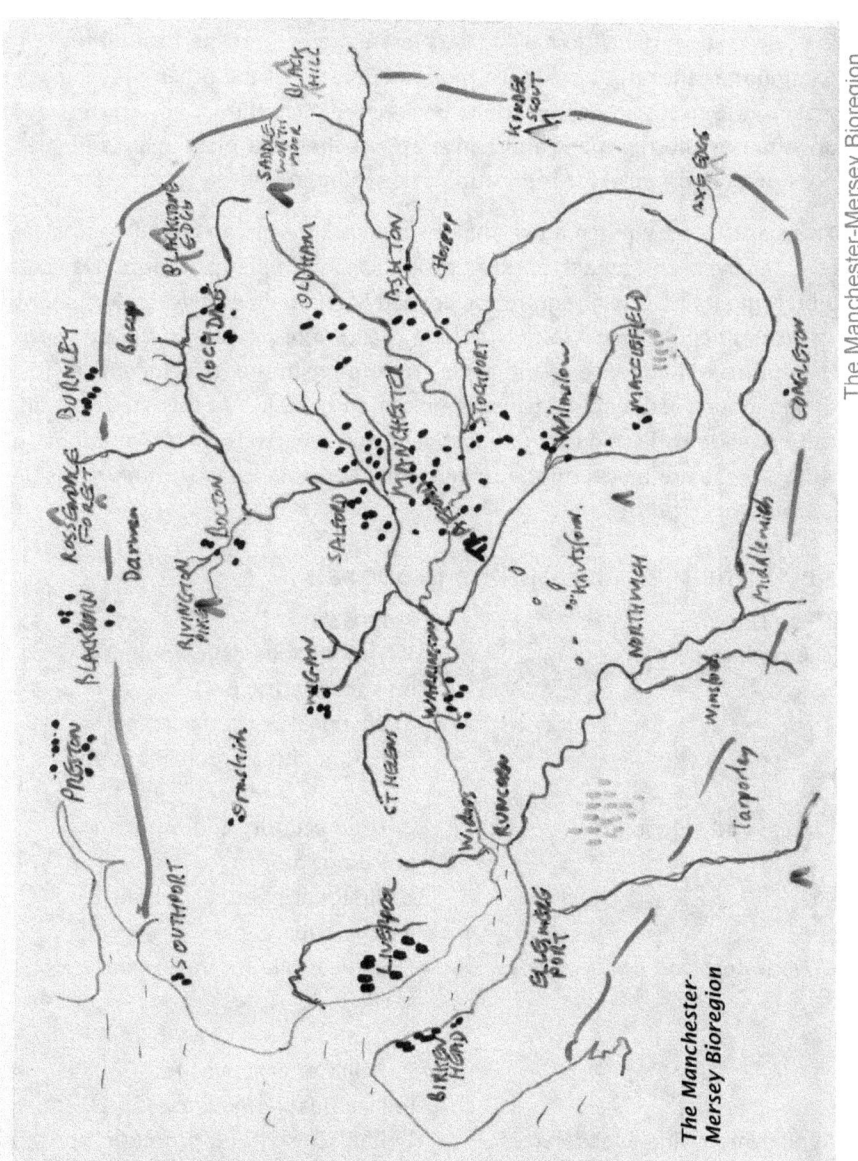

The Manchester-Mersey Bioregion

This initiative is not meant to be an alternative to the work going on regarding 'transition towns' but rather as a necessary complement to that approach. If there is a difference it is in terms of ambition: the triple challenge and especially that of climate change, is so urgent and immense in scale that we really do have to accelerate action, moving beyond the communitarian, rather anarchist modus operandi of the green movement, making the necessary connections between mainstream policy and governance and the many alternative approaches that offer images of possibility and nuclei for replication and scaling up.

This paper is very much a preliminary sketch, offering an overall 'high level' analysis and a pack of ideas for policy and implementation. However, a bioregional NGD will require the collective and deliberative work of many – stakeholders, experts, activists. The coalition of people working towards this future will increase as the triple crisis intensifies and as incentives for endogenous sustainable development get embedded. At this stage a start can be made by listing (not exhaustively) key proposals for a bioregional NGD. These are based on the underpinning criteria listed in *Appendix 2: Criteria for Action*.

Key principles and outline proposals

Theme	Proposals
The replacement economy	1) Endogenous development based on subsidiarity, p.6.
	4) Sustainable transport, p.11.
	05) Stimulate a green economy p.14.
Protect and safeguard	2) Food security and other shock-proofing, p.6.
	6) Safeguard and decarbonise energy supply, p.15.
Government and policy	7) Critical role for government, p.18.
	8) Public sector role, p.19.
	9) Policy alternatives for unsustainable industries, p.20.
Replacement financial services	3) Rediscovery and promotion of mutualism and cooperation, p.10.
Publicity and education.	10) Promote and educate, p.20.

1) **Endogenous economic development based on a principle of subsidiarity, linked to a regional de-globalising strategy.** This means

building up local and ecologically sustainable production and distribution for need in place of the sourcing of products and wealth sources on a global basis. Endogenous development[13] means development from within – in this case from within the communities of the Manchester-Mersey bioregion. The North West Development Agency will, in time, need to see its primary objective and its function as supporting endogenous sustainable development[14]. The establishment of the Manchester City Region with increased autonomy (Budget Statement, April 2009) could also support this emphasis. However it must be stressed that endogenous development does mean a change of emphasis from global competition to relative regional self-reliance..

2) **Build up food security and other forms of shock-proofing.** In these remaining days of cheap food, globally sourced by means of the energy-subsidised agro-foodstuffs complex, it is difficult to see the essential fragility of our essential supply chains. Yet as we saw in mid 2008 when food prices rose rapidly (this time it seems largely as a result of speculation on foodstuffs) our communities are very vulnerable to increases in cost and reductions in availability of essentials[15]. There is also the potential for other sources of shock to the food chain – we depend on a small number of key staples with diminishing genetic variability, all potentially vulnerable to new or mutated diseases. And other systemic shocks will make our population vulnerable to cold, flood, poverty and epidemic, to name but the most obvious. So,

* Focus on local and diverse production of <u>food calories</u> within the region and on locality-based fruit and vegetable production.

* Fund land use surveys to identify land that could easily be brought into production[16] – a feel for the scale of this can be achieved by looking out of a train window between say

---

[13] The term is being used in Venezuela to describe local economic development supported by State aid.

[14] Already it has embraced the idea of sustainability (see http://www.nwregionalstrategy.com/) but this needs to become a fundamental principle, conditioning and indeed limiting its other emphases (e.g. economic growth and competition in a global marketplace).

[15] The fuel price campaign in 2000 had an almost immediate impact on food availability, see Nine Meals from Anarchy: Oil dependence, climate change and the transition to resilience, NEF, 2008, http://tinyurl.com/6j72rz

[16] To include toxicity assessments in former industrial areas.

Manchester Piccadilly and Stockport: look how much land is simply idle, how much is given over to lawns, as opposed to how much is cultivated for useful products.

Vegetable production within the Manchester conurbation: Glebelands, Sale.

☆ Reduce meat intake to the level of occasional treats, but extend free range production of poultry, pigs and woodland / poor land forage species.

☆ Concentrate a significant amount of food production close to and within population centres[17][18].

☆ Offer public and private unused land for allotments – link to a capacitation[19] programme drawing on skills of existing gardeners and horticulturalists.

☆ Promote and develop new food products adapted to local production – grey squirrels and rabbits, tree crops, snails – possibly quinoa. At the same time emphasise locally adapted food crops for calories and protein – oats, barley, potatoes, field peas and field/broad beans for example.

☆ Retrieve where possible locally adapted varieties of fruit and vegetables.

☆ Invest in low energy / low technology methods of food preservation for the winter.

---

[17] "We already know about city farms, but now we need to go further, and think of cities as farms." Andy Goldring, Permaculture Association ("Permaculture and Energy", Reforesting Scotland 35, Autumn / Winter 2006.)

[18] See http://globalpublicmedia.com/articles/657 for the example of Cuba which has already faced and survived an energy crunch.

[19] Combination of training and development of appropriate and productive methods.

* Where they are available, use the traditional skills of both the majority community and immigrant heritage communities - for example intensive vegetable production methods traditional to East Asia to complement traditional gardening / allotment cultivation.

* Develop multi-product systems, for example by making grants available for stacked orchard/poultry systems pork/woodlot areas, carp/duck ponds.

* Emphasise a dual quick-return and mid range benefit approach to investment to secure an alternative economic base for employment, production and distribution.
This means 1) investing in areas such as insulation that can quickly absorb many workers and produce quick reductions in fuel usage, and b) also investing in areas that will be slower to produce results but whose results will be profound in their impact or required later in the cycle of decarbonisation – e.g. setting up the infrastructure (breeding, training, manufacture of vehicles) for animal traction systems, research and development into more efficient wind and water power systems, technologies for virtual reality tourism, etc.

* Build robust systems to strengthen welfare. For example support the establishment of credit unions, legitimise more of the informal economy (set to expand in relative terms during a recession) ending the campaigns against welfare fraud and instead promoting the use of benefits to subsidise local economic production. Establish contingency plans for food rationing and to discourage hoarding in case scarcity becomes a problem.

* Cold-proof the housing stock. Expand grants for insulation and invest in workforce for energy conservation[20]. Assume both reduced incomes and higher fuel prices / scarcity so develop insulation projects based on bioregional / local sources, for example recycling of plastics and aluminium and use of wool

---

[20] And possibly add in the whitening of roofs at the same time see
http://www.guardian.co.uk/environment/2009/jan/16/white-paint-carbon-emissions-climate

and forestry products. New-build social housing to use heat pumps and maximise passive solar gain.

* Invest in re-use / repair / reclaim / recycle cooperatives to provide work and make necessary products affordable.

* Strengthen community based mutual aid and social responsibility. For example, on a rolling basis – starting with the most at risk areas, develop local committees on a street or block basis to monitor welfare of vulnerable people – on a 'just checking', mutual aid, first line of welfare defence model.

* Social and health services will need to consider ways of increasing resilience to safeguard the most vulnerable[21].

* Local emergency plans (at council level) must include some key new threats and conduct simulation and testing exercises on these and develop mitigation action proactively:
  - sea level rises / flooding
  - severe storm damage
  - heat wave
  - other extremes of weather
  - fuel outages

3) **Rediscover and promote mutualism and cooperation.** Given the exhaustion and discrediting of finance capital as the basis for banking and credit services for individuals and organisations, mutualism and cooperation become the main contender for an ethical and shock-proof alternative. Current government policy is to support the 'third sector'. There is scope for (re-)directing this support to building the replacement economy while safeguarding current public service systems (only change what is unsustainable). As more enterprises become threatened this is also a good time to increase industrial democracy to engage working people and their knowledge in what concerns them a lot more than shareholders.

* Mutualism is endogenous by design – based on people with a common (often local) interest, coming together to create an organisational basis for productive action and wealth creation.

* Local government to explore financing of green projects[22] and needed services by the issuing of local bonds[23].

---

[21] The 2009 NEF report: "Green Well Fair: Three economies for social justice" is silent on this issue.

- ★ Foster credit unions, ethical banks, municipal banks[24], co-operatives, time banks/LETS, barter, microcredit[25]. TheCWU initiative for the Post Bank[26] is one such initiative worthy of broad-based support.

- ★ Exploit the regional connection of the country's foremost ethical bank - the Co-operative Bank[27].

- ★ Keep wealth in the region - in the medium term as regional autonomy grows, establish controls on the outward flow of money (for example transfers within multinational companies, repatriation of profits - look at local taxation). However, import protectionism may be counter-productive and in any case unnecessary as energy cost rises in the mid term make trade subsidiarity economically cost efficient.

- ★ Explore the option of local currency, usable for selected products and services and local trade, de-linked from national and international finance systems.

4) **Invest in sustainable transport systems** to reduce carbon emissions and safeguard the local economic infrastructure from energy price shocks.

- ★ Reduce the need for people to travel with incentives to live near the workplace (or vice versa).

- ★ Feet first - walking and cycling. Develop improved human powered vehicles, e.g. lightweight bicitaxis, and collectively pedalled local 'minibuses'.

Cycle hire scheme, Paris

---

[22] The Local Government Association has called for more powers for councils to do just this – see http://www.lga.gov.uk/lga/aio/1509491.

[23] http://www.guardian.co.uk/commentisfree/2008/oct/02/localgovernment.creditcrunch

[24] Already happening - see http://www.publicservice.co.uk/news_story.asp?id=7878 on the Essex bank.

[25] However, it is important to avoid the illusion that microcredit alone is sufficient to guarantee a sufficient level of justice and development – for this reason we also stress the role of local government.

[26] http://post.cwu.org/page/s/postbank

[27] And keep them to the ethical task – they tried to interest me in a £2k loan today when I phoned with an enquiry about my account!

* Free public transport – for the first 3–5 miles.

* Parking restrictions around all schools and promote and extend safe routes to school, walking buses etc.

* Reduce the need for transport of goods by localised production and distribution – fund local analysis of supply chains in order to take action on wasteful produce contraflows[28]. Increase public understanding of the trade subsidiarity principle – in the medium term establish / lobby for an embodied carbon labelling scheme for all major trade items starting with food and building materials.

No more half measures: this is supposedly a cycle lane in Manchester.!

* Use financial incentives to take car parks out of use. Building on some of them will reduce the transportation demand from the suburbs, and others can be converted to garden patios, public squares, play areas and so on.

* Impose and *enforce* 20 mph speed limit on urban roads (5 – i.e. close to walking speed – in residential areas and maybe 30 on dual carriageways) to slow down car borne traffic, making it more advantageous to take the bus – which will overtake cars on the bus lane – or walk/cycle. Use all available measures to give the lowest priority to the car (The City of Manchester already has this in its transport hierarchy, but it does need strong implementation).

---

[28] Product contraflows (our term) take at least two forms. 1) Products (e.g. non-speciality cheese) are produced in area A and sold in area B while identical or equivalent products are produced in area B and sold in area A. 2) A product (e.g. milk) is produced in area A, processed in area B nad then taken back to area A for sale and consumption. For some shocking examples see the NEF Interdependence Report at http://tinyurl.com/dkcm7s .

* Require all new build housing to design out the car – for example by limiting on street parking to disabled people and making high charges for parking on the periphery of the estate area[29].

* Councils and other public bodies to invert mileage allowances (highest for cyclists, then decreasing with increased engine size/emission rating). Invest in teleconferencing links to reduce meetings requiring travel.

* Re-establish waterways for goods transport – using modern computerised supply chain analysis to ensure efficiency and minimise need for warehousing (but avoid just-in-time models for essentials such as food where the need is to build stockpiles to increase bioregional resilience).

* Invest and continue to seek national government investment in bus and rail – lobby for re-regulation of bus services.

* Deploy local Research and Development on low carbon transport innovations such as short range hydro powered flywheel buses.

* Establish home delivery services based on the existing milk delivery fleet. Encourage these firms to negotiate supply contracts for renewable electricity (already the case with the Metrolink tram system[30]).

* As traffic reduces re-establish animal-drawn transport for local goods deliveries and passenger services – e.g. ring and ride horse bus. *This proposal was seen by some readers of earlier drafts as so far from our current reality that it might scare off some readers. But consider, the combined scenarios of peak fossil hydrocarbons and of the pressing need to stop burning them anyway mean that such options do need serious evaluation – even if seems like going backwards in time. There are real issues to consider, however –would the carrying capacity of the bioregion's soils be sufficient after taking out human food production, timber production, biomass energy?[31]*

---

[29] See the example of the Vauban district in Freiburg, Germany: http://www.vauban.de/info/abstract.html

[30] http://www.pepesecenergyplanning.eu/archives/79 This is an example of a public intervention (by GMPTE) in a market system of energy supply, using the power of the public sector procurement to address market failure within the parameters of a system of competing suppliers.

[31] The use of draught animals for agriculture and for public transport in small towns and cities was one of a number of steps Cuba took when it had to deal with its politically created peak oil crisis in

☆ The region's tourist attractions could be offered via a new 'virtual tourism', for example using a combination of real time digital technology and 'proxy tourists' who would go where the distant tourist (for a fee) requested.

Older near zero carbon forms of transport might have to return

5) **Stimulate a green economy.**

The Centre for Climate Change Economics and Policy at LSE suggests that the fiscal stimulus to deal with the recession needs to be around 4% of GDP. Of this about 20% could reasonably be on green investment[32]. For Greater Manchester this latter amount equates to £600M (for the North West as a whole £1,113M and for the City of Manchester £400M). These figures can only be very broad guides (and it is not clear whether the LSE group are suggesting this is a one-of figure, based as it is on the annual GDP), but they do give an indication of the scale of investment needed following fairly orthodox assumptions about the economy. Meanwhile studies have been conducted on the feasibility of establishing photovoltaic[33] and eco-remanufacturing[34] industries within the region. From our perspective the key elements (which overlap with other sections of this paper) are:-

☆ Promote green industries

☆ Fund Green R&D

---

the early 1990s. Luckily for them oxen were still used for ploughing on steep gradients and small fields in western Cuba and in flat small towns like Cárdenas horse buses had persisted in use. There was therefore a nucleus that could be used as a basis for reintroduction and for the necessary training in these methods.

[32] An outline of the case for a 'green' stimulus http://tinyurl.com/dllsjx The authors include Nicolas Stern who carried out the government's review of climate change and economy.

[33] http://www.urbed.coop/journals_show.php?j_id=76

[34] http://www.urbed.coop/journals_show.php?j_id=77

* Develop plans for the replacement of eco-destructive industry, where possible using skills, resources in sustainable ways.

* Refocus the Northern Way[35] project on endogenous trade subsidiarity-based developments, de-emphasising the Liverpool to Hull transport infrastructure elements (which will at best have only a short life due to the energy crunch and need to put fossil fuels beyond use).

* Given the need to reduce the carbon content of the atmosphere, local universities could be funded to identify, pilot and evaluate economic models for carbon sequestration integrated with agriculture (possibly charcoal burying).

* Public works initiatives including massive insulation programme (see NEF New green Deal) and re-forestation of marginal land with useful species for timber production[36].

6) **Safeguard and decarbonise energy supply.** Planning[37] is needed on several linked fronts to reduce unnecessary energy demand, develop alternative non-fossil fuel-based energy sources, cap and reduce the availability of fossil-fuel sources, plan for managing energy shocks as price/scarcity impacts[38]. The key here is to plan for interchangeability in supply, both *successively* over time – for example substituting fossil gas with biogas and oil-based electricity generation with tidal, and also *episodically*, for example by complementing wind and solar energy generation (for example in powering heat pumps).

* Each local authority to develop a heat plan, recognising that a large part of energy expenditure is used for water and space heating (80% on current stock, less on new build). This would include the use of both combined heat and power and district heating[39].

---

[35] http://www.nwda.co.uk/what-we-do/policy-and-strategy/northern-way.aspx
[36] Demand for and price of timber will soar with oil scarcity and cost.
[37] i.e. energy descent planning.
[38] The Tradable Energy Quota approach is not discussed here since this would require national level legislation. However bodies in the bioregion could lobby for it.
[39] In Denmark 60% of space heating is now provided via district heating – mostly as a result of retrofit. See Community Energy, Urban Planning for a Low Carbon Future. Manchester: URBED, TCPA and CHPA, 2008. http://www.urbed.coop/journals_show.php?j_id=134

* Stimulate local energy production using wind, solar, geothermal, hydro (including tidal[40] and wave) and sustainable biomass. Provide subsidies for green energy start-ups. Relax planning rules for renewable energy plant such as wind farms. Link reforestation with the development of biomass energy solutions[41] and energy co-ops - subject to prior impact assessment.

* Initiatives to reduce energy consumption. The NEF NGD emphasises an ambitious programme of public insulation works. Further initiatives could include subsidies and loans for low energy use appliances, supply chain analysis to exclude wasteful journeys, and the other proposals for example on transport elsewhere in this paper.

* Consider establishing an energy partnership with energy suppliers on the London model[42] to actively plan for decentralisation of energy supply.

* The mainstream idea of the energy coast of the NW region needs examination: it emphasises the nuclear industry and indeed the 48page executive summary[43] only mentions renewables once. There will probably have to be tidal installations to meet demand even with a reduction of overall energy demand[44]. There will likewise need to be investment in on and off shore wind generation. However the expansion of nuclear energy remains unproven and risky, although possibly least worst if the alternative is going to be substitution of fluid hydrocarbons with coal products[45]. The projections in the Zero Carbon Britain

---

[40] The Mersey has the second highest tidal range in the UK – 10m.

[41] The Jean Pain method is a neglected yet promising technology, inherently linked to forest stewardship and soil repair http://www.permacultureactivist.net/PeterBane/Jean_Pain.html and http://www.appropedia.org/Jean_Pain_system.

[42] In Action Today to Protect Tomorrow: The Mayor's Climate Change Action Plan. http://www.london.gov.uk/mayor/environment/climate-change/ccap/

[43] Britain's energy coast: a Masterplan for West Cumbria – executive summary. NWDA 2007. http://www.nwda.co.uk/pdf/WCSM_Summary(Final)%20(2).pdf

[44] Given the density of water and the reliability of the tides this is a particularly promising technology and it does not necessarily have to involve barrages (see the new Strangford Lough scheme in County Down for example http://www.guardian.co.uk/environment/2008/jul/17/waveandtidalpower.renewableenergy).

[45] The NWDA paper (http://www.nwda.co.uk/publications/infrastructure/britains-energy-coast.aspx) is only concerned with the East Cumbrian coast – outside the Manchester-Mersey bioregion, but a significant investment in large scale renewables there and on the Lancashire coast would be very significant for the Manchester-Mersey bioregion.

report[46] do not require a contribution from nuclear power and as bioregional MP Michael Meacher has argued[47], uranium too has already passed global peak production. It is likely that the nuclear contribution would arrive too late anyway to make a serious contribution to reducing the scale of climate change[48].

* Adopt progressively reducing carbon production caps at source. This will require legislation. It applies chiefly to the petrochemical industries – import and refinery in particular, but also gas and coal imports. It should be possible to identify the net import of hydrocarbons into the region and pinpoint where this is accounted for providing licences to sell hydrocarbons with a fixed and annually diminishing cap. This is a more likely to be effective than carbon trading at the point of consumption[49].

* Provide an energy survey and supplier accreditation service, which could be similar to the London Green Homes Concierge[50] service – but not necessarily limited to housing and with free surveys for people whose fuel costs are more than say 10% of household income.

* Subsidise and roll out smart metering, beginning with social housing.

* Review options for pumped storage schemes (to store renewable energy for use at peak demand times) within the bioregion using already existing reservoir chains, such as in the Goyt valley[51].

---

[46] Zero Carbon Britain. An alternative energy strategy http://www.zerocarbonbritain.com/
[47] http://tinyurl.com/d5gmxt
[48] Mirage and Oasis: Energy choices in an age of global warming, NEF, 2005, http://tinyurl.com/52j4rc
[49] See Harper, P. Clean Slate, no. 71, Spring 2009.
[50] www.greenhomesconcierge.co.uk
[51] Probably in combination with vehicle to grid storage – under trial in Bornholm, Denmark.

✷ Install micro-hydro schemes on Pennine slopes and other suitable sites (this can include canal locks).

The Goyt valley with the Erwood and Fernilee reservoirs, potential storage but in an area yet to begin the harvesting of wind.

✷ Use the region's sewage as a hydrocarbon and fertiliser source, aiming for 100% utilisation within 5 years.

✷ Provide facilitation and incentives for community based energy generation projects – a model already successfully developed on a large scale in Denmark[52] and on a small scale in the UK.

✷ Place an immediate ban on the burning of mooreland on the bioregion's upland areas: this exposes and oxidises peat, contributing considerably to emissions. Fund public works to safeguard and restore the upland blanket bogs as significant carbon sinks.

7) **There is a critical role for government and local government[53] which will have to lead and coordinate across the bioregion,** something that cannot be left to ad hoc arrangements[54]. This includes local councils, AGMA and collaborative arrangements (e.g. GMWDA, GMPTE), the Regional Government Office, the NHS – which already has a climate change plan[55], police, the various arms of the national state (e.g.

---

[52] see note 39.

[53] See TUC report: Unlocking Green Enterprise
http://www.tuc.org.uk/touchstone/unlocking/unlockinggreenenterprise.pdf

[54] While bottom up approaches are integral to endogenous and sustainable development, alone they do not amount to a strategy for transformation which will require top-down coordination of strategy and resource re-allocation.

[55] Saving Carbon, Improving Health: NHS Carbon Reduction Strategy for England.
http://www.sdu.nhs.uk/page.php?area_id=2

DWP/Job Centre Plus), the North West Development Agency which needs to adopt a specifically green mandate emphasising sustainable and endogenous economic development.

* One dimension of this is the promotion of a caring economy – not just based on the existing welfare system but moving the whole economy to a care for people model with production and distribution for need and sharing of resources paramount.

* Lobby for sustainability impact assessment in planning regulation and establish local policy frameworks to support sound planning choices.

* Engage civil society organisations as ways of involving people with high levels of social responsibility and energy in what will become an over-arching regional project.

* Use specific council tax and business tax incentives – e.g. rebate for insulation.

* Encourage firms to place car parking costs on employees by immediate reduction of the business rate component for car parking.

* Use building regulations to specify higher standards of insulation and an increasing proportion of re-used materials. Establish a construction waste disposal scheme, re-using all surplus and pre-used materials are put to use and using wood that cannot be reused as fuel.

* Conduct energy and climate vulnerability assessments and prepare and implement action plans based on them.

8) **The public sector more broadly has a major role to play,** and an increasing one as the economy shrinks. It will lead a new style of critical engagement with capital and markets rather than subservience to them. Where capital and market models deliver investment and efficiency that is not available through other sources then there is no reason to not engage, provided safeguards can be built in. Still unfashionable models of nationalised industry (and joint ventures with a majority public stake) and other forms of public and social ownership will likely enjoy a resurgence as the market-capital model becomes increasingly discredited. Public ownership

and joint ventures with a public stake will increase the accountability of the economy to the interests of the people. The public sector will also provide a significant buffer for the possibly sudden collapse of the current trade based economy. In the medium term improved democratic governance will be needed – especially as central control loosens.

9) **Policy alternatives need establishing for the region's key unsustainable industries such as the airports, retail malls and those sectors dependent on the sale and servicing of private motorised transport.**

   * Phased scaling back with funding for retraining and replacement employment[56].

   * Carry out feasibility studies for reorientation of skills and support industries.

   * A moratorium on new investment in energy intensive / energy squandering schemes.

10)   **Promote, educate and build community solidarity.**

   * Use local media to mirror key ideas, building support and understanding for what will be unfamiliar changes in a challenging environment. Promote positive stories about the new initiatives.

   * Ensure that sections of the population do not become scapegoats, for example by presenting positive stories of the contribution of ethnic and other minority communities and groups to building the replacement economy. Meanwhile anti–fascist activism will be increasingly crucial.

   * Spread know–how necessary in a low carbon social and economic system, for example by using adult education and colleges to offer "how to" courses on all aspects of living under conditions of post–affluence. Grants could also be given to community and green groups for this work.

---

[56] Again the much maligned Cuban State has shown how this can be done with its large scale downsizing of the sugar production and refining industry.

* Business schools to offer capacitation[57] to local entrepreneurs as part of endogenous strategy for the region – using models such as the Brazilian *Organisational Workshop*[58].

* Establish a network of neighbourhood transition champions as points for advice and support for people 'down-powering'.

* Find ways to promote an ethic of 'necessary use' rather than the reckless consumption of the last few decades[59]. This involves helping us all to regain a sense of self and identity that is based on mutualism, respect, responsibility, solidarity, sense of place – in short social ties and connectedness and not on the stuff we've got or the extravagance of our last holiday or night out.

A more sustainable urban environment: the Homes for Change housing co-op and community garden centre, Hulme, Manchester.

[57] See note 19

[58] Carmen, R (2000) *A Future for the Excluded: Job Creation and Income Generation by the Poor Clodomir Santos De Morais and the Organizational Workshop.* London: Zed Books

[59] The very term 'consume' suggests using something once, so destroying it.

Afterword: some of this has already happened.

"In the early 1990s we were desperate to find practical alternatives to large-scale food production. It was urgent. We found and developed vacant municipal lots for organic agriculture. This was the start of our urban farming experiment. It was based upon need and it found resonance amongst residents. Ill-fated are cities that do not include urban plots in their agendas." – Conrado Martinez, Mayor of the City of Havana, 1999

Cuban permaculturalist, Roberto Pérez shares lessons from Cuba's work on furban food security with a Machester audience, September, 2008.

Appendix 1: The NEF *New Green Deal*, its proposals.

The NEF Green New Deal –combines stabilisation in the short term with longer–term restructuring of the financial, taxation and energy systems. It aims to be international in outlook, requiring action at local, national, regional and global levels.

At the UK national level the authors propose an interlocking programme consisting of:

* A programme of investment in a low–carbon energy system that will include making 'every building a power station'. Involving tens of

millions of properties, their energy efficiency will be maximised, as will

the use of renewables to generate electricity.

* Creating and training a 'carbon army' of hundreds of thousands workers to provide the human resources for a vast environmental reconstruction programme. It will be part of a wider shift from an economy narrowly focused on financial services and shopping to one that is an engine of environmental transformation.

* Ensuring more realistic fossil fuel prices that include the cost to the environment, and are high enough to tackle climate change effectively by creating the economic incentive to drive efficiency and bring alternative fuels to market. This includes establishing an Oil Legacy Fund, paid for by a windfall tax on the profits of oil and gas companies to help deal with the effects of climate change and smooth the transition to a low–carbon economy.

* Developing a wide–ranging package of other financial innovations and incentives to assemble the tens of billions of pounds that need to be spent on the development of new, efficient energy infrastructure and also help reduce demand for energy, particularly among low–income groups,

for example by improving home insulation

* Re–regulating the domestic financial system to ensure that the creation of money at low rates of interest is consistent with democratic aims, financial stability, social justice and environmental sustainability.

* Breaking up the discredited financial institutions by a forced de–merger of large banking and finance groups. Retail banking should be split from both corporate finance (merchant banking) and from securities dealing.

* Re–regulating and restricting the international finance sector to transform national economies and the global economy. Finance will have to be returned to its role as servant,

not master, of the global economy, to dealing prudently with people's savings and providing regular capital for productive and sustainable investment.

* Subjecting all derivative products and other exotic instruments to official inspection and approval to facilitate a planned scaling down of the financial sector in relation to the rest of the economy.

* Minimising corporate tax evasion by clamping down on tax havens and corporate financial reporting. International accounting rules should be changed to eliminate transfer mispricing by requiring corporations to report on a country-by-country basis. These measures will provide much-needed sources of public finance at a time when economic contraction is reducing conventional tax receipts.

The UK should also promote the following:

* Allowing all nations far greater autonomy over domestic monetary policy (interest rates and money supply) and fiscal policy (government spending and taxation).

* Setting a formal international target for atmospheric greenhouse gas concentrations that keeps future temperature rises as far below 2°C as possible.

* Delivering a fair and equitable international climate agreement to succeed the Kyoto Protocol in 2012.

* Giving poorer countries the opportunity to escape poverty without fuelling global warming by helping to finance massive investment in climate-change adaptation and renewable energy.

* Supporting the free and unconstrained transfer of new energy technologies to developing countries.

Appendix 2: Criteria for Action

The following criteria are suggested to guide the selection of action proposals. In principle they could be quantified in order to choose between competing courses of action.

* Reduces carbon emissions
* Builds on regional assets.
* Keeps wealth in the region.
* Meets the needs of local people.
* Builds social solidarity / social capital / community / mutual aid.
* Is feasible using proven or emergent technologies (material or social).
* Is proportionate to the scale of the enormous triple challenges – either alone or in conjunction with other proposals.

Appendix 3: What are the crises and what has caused them?

There are various ways of describing the crises and their interrelations, but an adequate approach will have to go right to the roots[60]. For this we need to take a long view and try to understand the dominant economic system under and within which the majority of the earth's population now lives[61].

Underpinning everything is an economic and social system that for some 200 years has efficiently created an explosion in production, access to goods and commodities, technological sophistication, population, longevity and knowledge. The motor for this has been capital, something that within this system has the propensity to increase. That increase in Capital[62] is based fundamentally on exploitation – of workers, consumers and natural resources. The continued expansion of Capital is fraught with limiting factors – the tendency of the rate of profit to fall with technical innovation, the over-capacity of the productive forces (in relation to consumption, particularly as at the same time there is a drive to keep wages down) and the problem of absorbing and re-investing ever growing capital. Yet the system has proved immensely adept at overcoming these *internal* contradictions – **until now**.

We can identify distinct phases of capitalist evolution and the fixes that Capital has found to keep on expanding. This is inevitably a simplified picture.

1) *Classical industrial capitalism* of the 19th and early 20th century. Fixes included exploitation of the first 'energy subsidy' – coal, and colonial administration to suppress competition (e.g. Indian cotton, Irish corn) and find new markets.

---

[60] The emphasis here on Capital and its inexorable expansion is perhaps a corrective against some analyses that see the problem as residing in the market model *per se*. Our position is that coordination by markets has its place (great for barber shops and restaurants, for example) as does coordination by the State and by associations (such as co-operatives and communities). While market failure is an explanation for some aspects of the current triple crisis, our analysis suggests that the problem is more fundamental. Indeed some market tools will be invaluable in combating climate change and peak energy.

[61] This analysis is broadly a green Marxist one. However we have to acknowledge that while the insights of Marx and contemporary Marxist scholars are a rich resource for analysis of the system as it is and as it has developed, they offer less help with defining a future sustainable, non-exploitive social and economic system. For that urgent task it is necessary to draw on a wider set of ideas.

[62] Capital (with a capital 'C') refers here to a cohesive subsystem in society comprised of both capital in economic terms *and* the actions, strategy, ideology of those who work to increase the accumulation of capital – its production and reproduction and expansion. These people were initially the classical industrial capitalists of the 19th Century, but over the last 100 years the function has been to greater or lesser extent become systemic in nature, with the development of professions such as accountancy and the establishment of bodies such as pension funds and corporate bonds that function objectively as the capitalist.

2) *Fordist industrial capitalism*. Fixes included the use of cheap immigrant labour, new energy subsidies (petroleum), the development of new markets and new lines of production and the rationalisation of the labour process on Fordist lines.

3) *Welfare capitalism*. After the great anti-fascist war of 1939–45 a compromise was made with the labour movement, trading off welfare subsidies via the State for Trade Union militancy and radical system change. However as a result of this accommodation Capital was able to externalise some of the 'reproduction costs' (e.g. education and welfare of the workforce) to the welfare system. Further technological innovations and expanded energy subsidies (including nuclear power) also fed this as did the continued expansion of global markets and resource extraction (post colonialism).

4) *Neoliberal phase of capitalism* (a.ka. globalisation, post-Fordism). When the post war settlement began to break down (exacerbated by the 1974 oil shock), Capital again adapted by means of a set of linked strategies that all had roots in the earlier phases. The fixes this time included

- $ Restriction of Trade Union power by (depending on location) violence, legislation and the harnessing of State power to capital interests.
- $ Privatisation of socially owned functions and enterprises – creating new sites for capital creation and accumulation.
- $ Outsourcing of production (and some other functions) to cheap labour economies.
- $ Dual process of extortion and control of non-core system economies via economic and military warfare, leading to the collapse of the soviet block (which besides opening up a huge new terrain for Capital also weakened alternatives and opposition in the rest of the world for some 30 years), the subordination and integration of dependent economies into the global system through the now neoliberally modelled Bretton Woods institutions (World Bank, International Monetary Fund and its regional proxies, and the World Trade Organisation), along with bilateral and multilateral trade agreements (e.g. NAFTA).
- $ Associated with the above, resource wars, whether direct (Iraq) or by proxy (Congo).
- $ The hyper-development of finance capital. Banking became in its own right a site for capital accumulation rather than an aid to the smooth working of the productive economy. There was the transfer of State and mutual resources to private capital, the de-regulation of the system and then the recursive growth of finance capital via secondary products –

27

derivatives, unsecured debt and associated bundling: a finance bubble that as we know has just crashed dramatically, plunging the rest of the global economy into free fall.

$ New commodities and the extension of market mechanisms to more areas providing a terrain for the operations of Capital.

The economic system as a whole can be thought of in three parts[63]. Starting in the middle:–

A real economy[64] of production with a motor of capital and steering mechanisms of market and government – *economy 2*.

An unreal finance economy – that grew larger than the real economy, developed autonomously from it and which we now know was no more than a speculative bubble – like those in previous stages of capitalist evolution – *economy 1*.

Underpinning everything, an earth economy based on the natural processes of the ecosystem and the fundamental cycles that structure it – water, nitrogen, carbon, oxygen – all powered by sunlight – *economy 3*.

Economy 1 presents a short–range problem. Its explosion has meant the destruction or at least severe damage to the financial tools – banking, savings and credit – that underpin *economy 2*.

Economy 2 sprouted *economy 1* as one of Capital's solutions to its *internal* constraints (basically the inherent tendency of the rate of profit to fall). But it also faces some other constraints that are fatally limiting: the crisis of *economy 3*. The most important of these is firstly the increasing scarcity in the form of fluid hydrocarbons (oil and gas) – peak oil. And this constraint arrives at the same moment that we learn decisively that (secondly) we cannot afford to increase carbon emissions and indeed need year by year reductions to mitigate the impact of the now present and inevitable change in global climate. This can only mean living on greatly reduced energy inputs. So the real economy, <u>currently</u> structured by an intrinsically expansionist motor of capital accumulation, has reached its limits to growth and needs to be

---

[63] This idea comes from JM Alier La crisis económica, vista desde la economía ecológica. http://www.ecoportal.net/content/view/full/82771/://

[64] Distinctions made here are relative. The finance economy is also real in the sense that it is a material construction – the distinction is that the economy of production deals with physically material things rather than abstract entities. However, as Marx showed, the concepts that every day structure this real economy also have an abstract and ideological quality.

restructured on the basis of production for need on an ecologically sustainable basis.

Allied to the crisis of *economy 3* is the food crisis – itself a product of the energy and financial crises – and the population crisis, less a cause of the ecological crisis *per se*[65] but an index of probably unsatisfiable human want. Let us be clear, these crises are killing people and they will kill many more of us yet.

So the conjuncture of crises can be summarised in the following terms:

1) Financial crisis.

Requires a complete restructuring of the financial sector, with a return to its basic functions for any economy – provision of banking, savings and credit facilities, either on a social ownership basis, or if profit is to be made, at least it should be at a rate commensurate with the real sums invested.

This crisis can be fixed by action at local, regional, national and international levels. *It is not enough to re-regulate the financial system – it needs a thorough rebuild.*

2) Energy crisis.

The increasing shortage of hydrocarbon fuels – initially in the case of the fluid fuels gas and oil. *This will have impact on all other sectors and means an austerity energy budget.*

3) Climate crisis.

The urgent need to decarbonise the economy. This means that in addition to facing the energy cost problem, action is needed now to progressively put the vast majority of fossil carbon fuel *beyond use.*

4) Economic crisis

This is the product of the three forgoing crises and of the internal contradictions of the present governance (or lack of it) of the real economy. Responding to this requires more than a return to a Keynesian demand management model – albeit a green version. For this reason **a Green New Deal has to be based on localisation / trade subsidiarity, and production and distribution for need.**

4) Food crisis.

The energy crisis, with the climate crisis, makes food security a pressing priority for a country that is a net importer of food. Basically we eat oil: we

---

[65] WWF Living Planet Report, 2008.

are dependent on high energy subsidies to cultivate, harvest, distribute, store and prepare our food. The energy and climate crises mean likely hunger.

The context for action

The present unprecedented combination of crises presents both an enormous challenge, but also an unexpected opportunity.

The challenge is a result of the crises. It means the stakes have never been higher. The collapse of the financial systems makes it difficult to mobilise the investments needed to safeguard our population and transform the carbon economy – that is to make the transition. Moreover, many of the needed changes will seem like going back to a more primitive way of life with more physical labour and fewer luxuries.

An opportunity, though, is also present in the combination of crises. Because the dominant system is so obviously broken, minds and energies are more likely to be open and ready to address the challenge with the radical vigour that is required. While action needs to take place on all levels from the international down to the domestic, it is our view that the bioregional level holds the key to the most significant redesign of our settlements and the way we live in them.

Appendix 4: Key assumptions of transition initiatives.

From Hopkins (2008) The Transition Handbook: From Oil Dependency to Local resilience p. 134.

1. Life with drastically lower energy consumption is inevitable.

2. It is better to plan for it than to be taken by surprise.

3. Our settlements and communities presently lack the resilience to enable them to weather the severe energy shocks that will accompany peak oil.

4. We have to act collectively and act now.

5. By unleashing the collective genius of those around us to creatively and proactively design our energy descent, we can build ways of living that are more connected, more enriching and that recognise the biological limits of the planet.

Note, in the original, assumptions 1 and 2 are combined.

 Find more information, relevant links and comments at
http://greendealmanchester.wordpress.com/

Email: contactgdm@googlemail.com

version 4.5, October 2009

A New Green Deal for the Manchester–Mersey Bioregion was written by Mark Burton, April 2009.